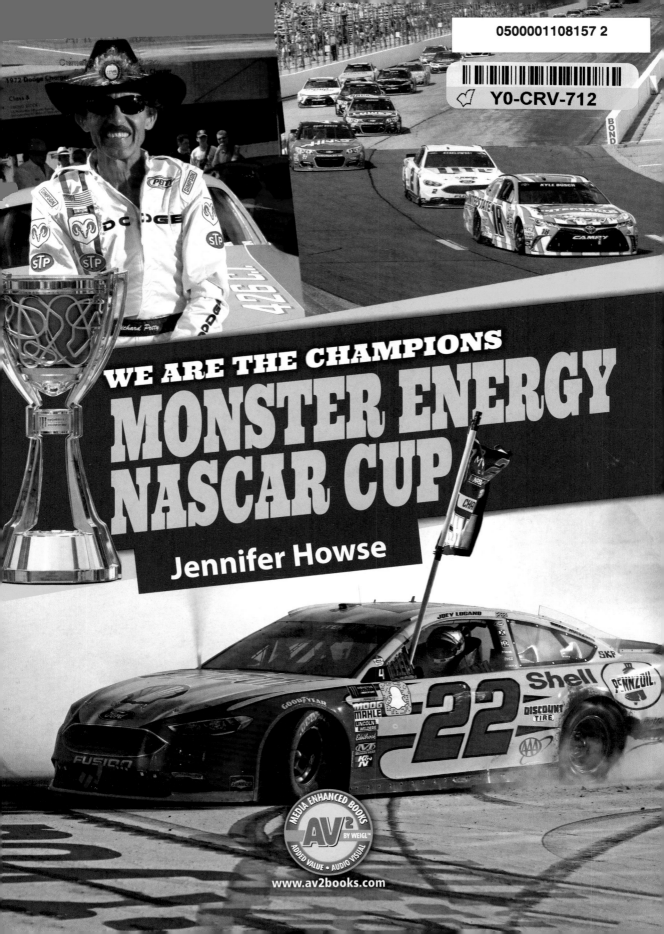

WE ARE THE CHAMPIONS
MONSTER ENERGY NASCAR CUP

Jennifer Howse

MEDIA ENHANCED BOOKS
AV2 BY WEIGL
ADDED VALUE · AUDIO VISUAL

www.av2books.com

MEDIA ENHANCED BOOKS

AV² BY WEIGL™

ADDED VALUE • AUDIO VISUAL

AV² provides enriched content that supplements and complements this book. Weigl's AV² books strive to create inspired learning and engage young minds in a total learning experience.

Your AV² Media Enhanced books come alive with...

Audio
Listen to sections of the book read aloud.

Key Words
Study vocabulary, and complete a matching word activity.

Video
Watch informative video clips.

Quizzes
Test your knowledge.

Embedded Weblinks
Gain additional information for research.

Slide Show
View images and captions, and prepare a presentation.

Try This!
Complete activities and hands-on experiments.

... and much, much more!

Go to **www.av2books.com**, and enter this book's unique code.

BOOK CODE

A V F 5 5 7 7 8

AV² by Weigl brings you media enhanced books that support active learning.

Published by AV² by Weigl
350 5th Avenue, 59th Floor
New York, NY 10118
Website: www.av2books.com

Library of Congress Control Number: 2018965265

ISBN 978-1-7911-0041-4 (hardcover)
ISBN 978-1-7911-0578-5 (softcover)
ISBN 978-1-7911-0043-8 (single-user eBook)
ISBN 978-1-7911-0042-1 (multi-user eBook)

Printed in Brainerd, Minnesota, United States
1 2 3 4 5 6 7 8 9 0 22 21 20 19 18

122018
102318

Project Coordinator: Jared Siemens
Art Director: Terry Paulhus

Every reasonable effort has been made to trace ownership and to obtain permission to reprint copyright material. The publishers would be pleased to have any errors or omissions brought to their attention so that they may be corrected in subsequent printings. Weigl acknowledges Getty Images and Alamy as its primary image suppliers for this title.

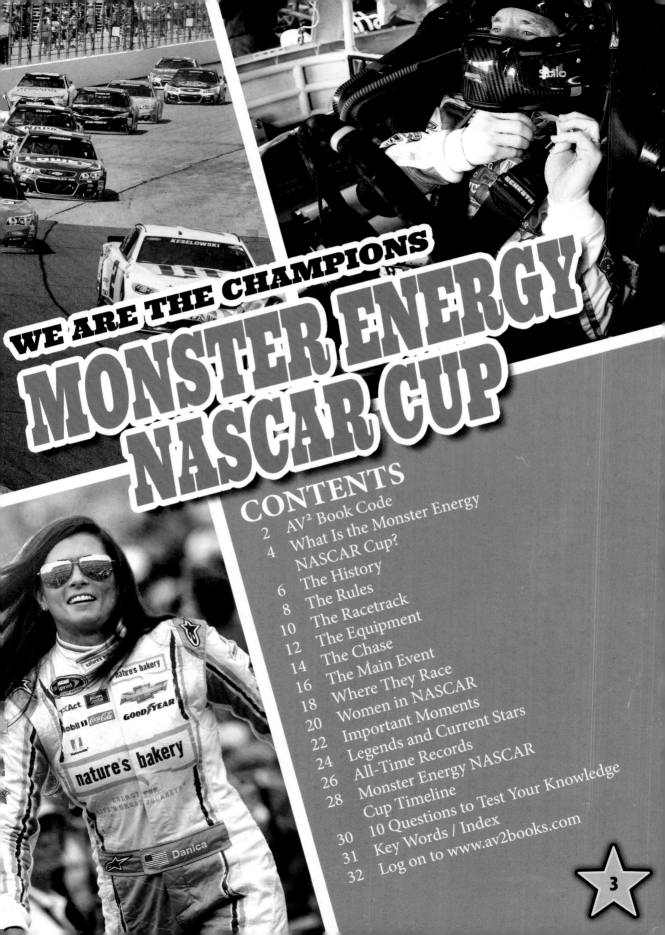

WE ARE THE CHAMPIONS

MONSTER ENERGY NASCAR CUP

CONTENTS

3

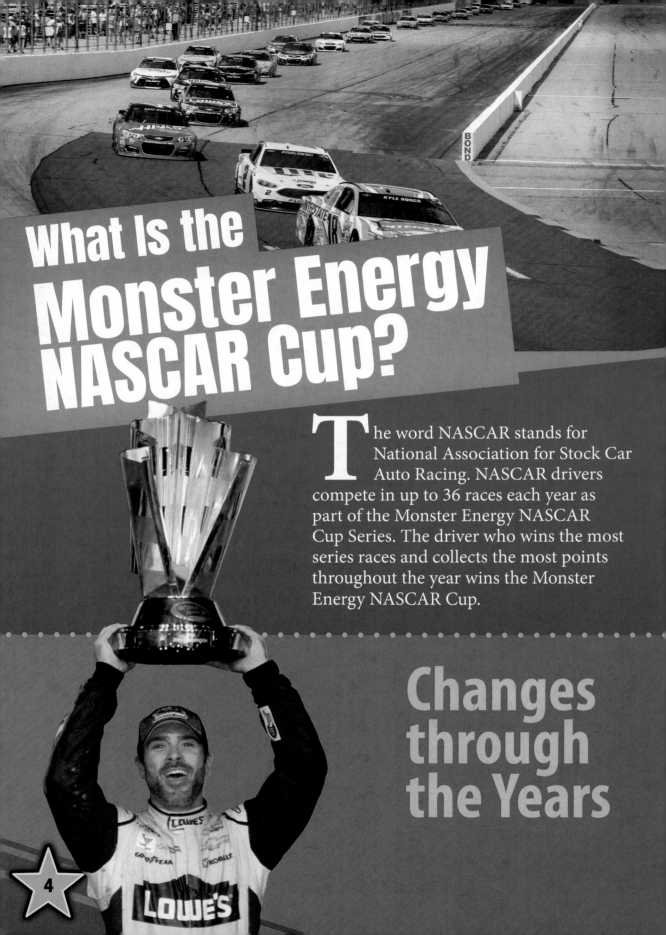

What Is the Monster Energy NASCAR Cup?

The word NASCAR stands for National Association for Stock Car Auto Racing. NASCAR drivers compete in up to 36 races each year as part of the Monster Energy NASCAR Cup Series. The driver who wins the most series races and collects the most points throughout the year wins the Monster Energy NASCAR Cup.

Changes through the Years

In a NASCAR race, 43 cars soar around a racetrack at speeds of up to 200 miles (322 kilometers) per hour. These competitions pit stock car drivers against each other on different types of racetracks. Cash prizes and a variety of off-track activities are a part of every race.

There may only be one person behind the wheel, but NASCAR is not a solo sport. Each driver is supported by dozens of people. A team is made up of owners, managers, crew members, and sponsors. They all work together to get drivers and their cars ready for race day.

Since 1948, NASCAR has become one of the most popular sports in the United States. Each year, millions of fans gather at racetracks to watch these high-octane events. Fans of all ages are thrilled by the sounds, sights, and excitement of NASCAR races. Spectators are encouraged to wear earplugs, as cars roaring down the track create as much noise as a jet engine. Fans can also bring binoculars to watch their favorite drivers and crews up close.

Richard Petty has won **200** races, more than any other driver.

Cars with the number 11 have won more races, **209**, than cars with any other numbers.

Bill Elliott set the NASCAR speed record of **212.809** miles (342.5 kilometers) per hour in 1987.

Additionally, the races are broadcast on television. It's not unusual for big races to attract more than 5 million viewers across the country. This opens up the world of stock car racing to many new prospective fans, ensuring NASCAR's continued popularity.

PAST	PRESENT
Regular cars with few changes made to the body and engine were used in races.	Drivers race cars that are made up of specially designed parts that fit strict specifications.
Races were held on oval-shaped dirt tracks.	Today's racetracks feature **asphalt** roadways on courses designed by engineers.
Several races were held over a single weekend.	Qualifying races throughout the week lead up to one main race on the weekend.
The top racing series was called the NASCAR Grand National.	The Monster Energy NASCAR Cup Series is currently the top stock car racing championship.

The History

At the turn of the twentieth century, automobiles were growing popular, and more and more people wanted to own and drive them. Cars offered people a chance to move quickly from one place to another. As new car technology developed, people began to gather and watch car races.

Interest in stock car racing grew rapidly during the 1920s and early 1930s. People began racing **unmodified** cars. It was not long before they started making changes to the cars so they could travel faster. Over time, they began racing these modified cars in their free time.

In 1936, the first organized stock car race in the United States was held in Daytona Beach, Florida. However, the race was called off because of incoming tides on the beach portion of the racecourse. In addition, the organizers did not arrive in time to sell any tickets, and they lost money on the event. In 1938, a Florida stock car racer and mechanic, Bill France, and a local restaurant owner named Charlie Reese took control of the event. They shared a small profit and held another event a month later. The two continued scheduling successful races, although they were forced to put them on hold once World War II (1939–1945) started.

By the 1940s, stock car racing was a common pastime for many Americans. Across the country, a number of groups formed to cater to the fans and drivers of this sport. It became clear that a national organization was needed to bring these groups under a common set of rules.

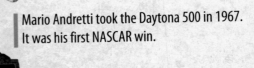

Mario Andretti took the Daytona 500 in 1967. It was his first NASCAR win.

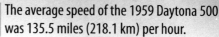
The average speed of the 1959 Daytona 500 was 135.5 miles (218.1 km) per hour.

Under Bill France's guidance, NASCAR was formed in 1948. The first Grand National Series was held in 1949, though it was called Strictly Stock until it was renamed for the 1950 season. The NASCAR Grand National Series, which later became the Monster Energy NASCAR Cup Series, included eight races on oval-shaped dirt tracks.

In 1971, the Grand National series became known as the Winston Cup. The following year, the number of races in a season was reduced to 31. By this time, stock cars had become purpose-built race cars rather than typical sedans.

In 1982, a new tradition was introduced to NASCAR races. From that time on, the first race of the series each year took place at the Daytona International Raceway. Daytona's weekend of races kicks off the NASCAR racing season with great fanfare every February. In 2003, Nextel became the series sponsor, but after partnering with a company called Sprint, the series was renamed the Sprint Cup Series in 2008. Energy drink company Monster Energy then purchased naming rights to the series in 2017.

MONSTER ENERGY NASCAR CUP SPONSORS

An important part of a NASCAR team is the team's sponsor. Drivers and **pit crews** must earn an income. Also, stock cars are extremely expensive to maintain, fuel, and repair. Sponsors pay drivers to take part in races. They provide key funding in exchange for the opportunity to have the driver and car display their company logos and colors. Placement of these logos is important, and the top sponsor has the privilege of having its company logo on the hood of the car.

The Rules

Since 1949, several rules have been established to ensure NASCAR races are fair and safe for drivers and pit crews. NASCAR **officials** conduct five inspections of each car—once before the first practice, before and after qualifying races, and immediately before and after the main race.

At the first race of the season at Daytona Speedway, a very thorough inspection is conducted to ensure cars are meeting guidelines for size, motors, and safety. This inspection sets a standard for the entire race season.

1

Car Engines

Engines are checked to see that they follow size guidelines and to ensure the **compression ratio** is correct. Until 2011, NASCAR vehicles had to use a carburetor. This is a special device that mixes air and gas for the engine to burn as it runs. In 2012, a rule change forced all Monster Energy NASCAR Cup cars to switch to a fuel injection system that sprays gas directly into the engine.

2

Body and Chassis

The body is the outside cover of the car. It is made from steel sheet metal. It must be a specific size and shape. The shape of the cars is based on designs by Ford, Chevrolet, Toyota, and Dodge. The car cover sits on top of the chassis, or frame. Roll bars are also an important part of the chassis. They are a type of cage that protects the driver if a rollover occurs.

3

Car Mechanics

Stock car tires are a standard size and must be completely smooth, with no **treads**. A special gas tank, or fuel cell, gives all the cars about the same gas mileage. The fuel cells hold 17.75 gallons (67.2 liters) of fuel, as this affects the speed and durability of the car. Fuel cells must be lined with foam rubber to prevent leaks.

4

Metal Parts

All of the metal parts of the car, such as the chassis, must be made from steel and not a lighter-weight material, such as titanium. Officials use a magnet as a way to test if the proper materials have been used in the **manufacturing** of the car. Magnets are attracted to steel parts, so the official can hold a magnet over the car parts to determine if they are steel.

5

Safety Checks

Safety belts, harnesses, and window nets are inspected to be sure they meet code. There are five belts that cross over each driver to hold them securely in place. These belts are made to snap open quickly in an emergency. Officials check the safety belts to be certain that the correct material was used in their construction. Window nets are used so that, in case of a crash, the driver does not fall through the window.

MAKING THE CALL

After a car has been inspected, officials decide if it is fit to take part in the race. If officials do not approve a car to race, they can ask the team to replace parts. If, after a second inspection, these parts are not suitable, the driver, team, or car owner may face penalties or elimination from the race.

Once the race has begun, there are no set rules for how drivers compete on the track. An unwritten code of conduct encourages drivers to treat each other with respect and courtesy. If drivers are risking the safety of others, they can be penalized.

The Racetrack

By the 1960s, only three dirt oval tracks were still in use. The last dirt-track race was held in 1970 in Raleigh, North Carolina. Since then, the series has been run on paved racetracks. Oval tracks less than 1 mile (1.6 km) long are called short tracks. Intermediate or speedway tracks are 1 to 2 miles (1.6 to 3.2 km) in length. Longer tracks, or superspeedways, are more than 2 miles (3.2 km) long. Road courses are less about length and more about the challenge presented by the twists and turns of each track.

On most NASCAR tracks, all of the turns are to the left. However, road course tracks have both left and right turns. These tracks are made to be like real roads.

Track speeds at a NASCAR race can vary depending on the length and shape of the track. Special features of the track can make it faster or slower to drive. If a racetrack has level, or flat, turns, it is a slower track. If the track has raised or inclined turns, called **banking**, it is a faster track. The Talladega Superspeedway in Alabama has the highest track banking in the Monster Energy NASCAR Cup Series, at a 33-degree angle. The tilted track lets drivers take turns at higher speeds.

DRIVING THE TRACK

Drivers race their cars at extremely fast speeds. Competing on the track involves shifting gears properly and moving the car around other cars to gain an advantage. Drivers often race in packs of three cars across a narrow stretch of track. Drivers in the packs that are leading the race do not want drivers from behind to pass them. The best time to pass is during a turn. Drivers behind other cars will stay very close to a leading car's bumper, waiting for a chance to move ahead. Tapping the front car on the bumper is a tactic used to move that car out of the way. If the lead drivers are much faster than the other cars in a race, they lap the slower cars on the track. This means that they have circled the track at least one full lap more than some of the slower drivers.

TALLADEGA SUPERSPEEDWAY

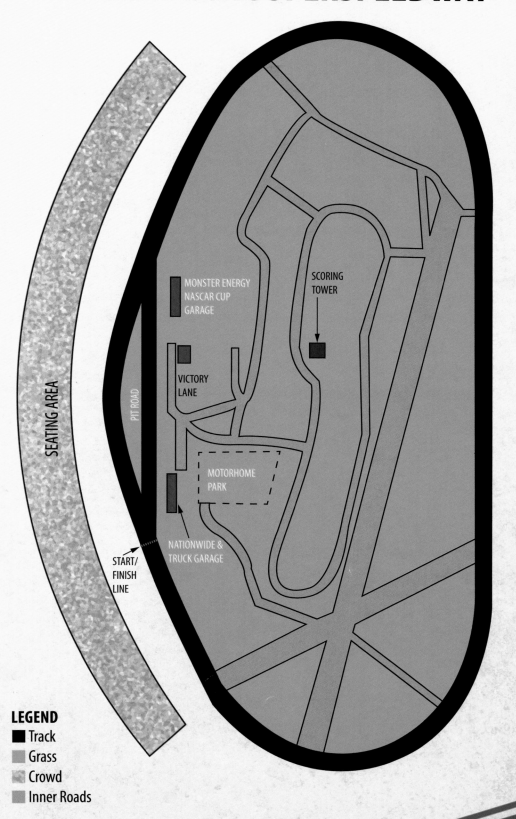

SEATING AREA

PIT ROAD

MONSTER ENERGY
NASCAR CUP
GARAGE

SCORING
TOWER

VICTORY
LANE

MOTORHOME
PARK

START/
FINISH
LINE

NATIONWIDE &
TRUCK GARAGE

LEGEND
- Track
- Grass
- Crowd
- Inner Roads

The Equipment

From the stands of a superspeedway, the crowd can hear the loud roar of the stock car engines as they speed around the track. Though they look like normal street cars, each of these race cars is specially designed for NASCAR. Engineers, physicists, mechanics, chemists, and car technology specialists all help to make NASCAR vehicles.

The first stock cars were bulky and heavy. Today, the cars are sleek and **aerodynamic** so that they can safely withstand great speeds. Each car weighs 3,400 pounds (1,542 kilograms), with a **wheelbase** of 110 inches (2.79 meters). Although the cars are made by different teams, there are some features that all stock cars must include, such as an eight-cylinder engine that is 358 cubic inches (5,867 cubic centimeters) in size.

Stock Car

Seat belt

Roll bar

Decals/logos

Engine

Stock cars are custom-made. This process involves shaping, forming, welding, and sealing the car. Once completed, paint is applied for a glossy finish, and decals are stuck onto the car. Inside, the car is light in color, except for the red fuel-line pipe. It is brightly colored so it can be found quickly if there is an emergency. There are three pedals on the floor—a gas pedal, a brake pedal, and a **clutch** pedal. The steering wheel must be set up specially for each driver.

Driver

Fire-resistant suit

Helmet

Shoes

SAFETY FIRST

NASCAR drivers are racing professionals. They work hard to learn the skills needed to drive cars at high speeds. They also use special equipment to help keep them safe. Drivers wear a fire-resistant, one-piece suit. The suit must let the driver move easily enough to steer and climb out of the car quickly in the case of an emergency. Drivers wear helmets that are made from materials that do not burn or melt. The helmet visor is made from a bulletproof material. Seat belts are made from tightly woven fabrics that do not stretch as much as those found in passenger cars. The seat belts are fitted to each driver.

The Chase

By the end of the 2003 NASCAR season, Matt Kenseth had more points than any of the other racers. It was known that he would win the Monster Energy NASCAR Cup even before the last races took place. As a result, people lost interest in watching those races. To prevent this from happening again, a new playoff point system was developed for the following season.

The Monster Energy NASCAR Cup Series is now divided into a regular season and the playoffs. This system was adopted in 2004 and updated in 2014. The playoffs, also called the Chase for the Cup, have four parts. This encourages competition throughout the year. After the first 26 races, the top 16 drivers qualify for the first round of the Chase. Rankings are determined by race wins, and drivers are awarded points based on their wins. After three races, the Chase enters its second phase, with only 12 drivers qualifying. After another three races, eight drivers qualify for the third phase. The last phase includes only four qualified drivers. They compete in the last three races of the season for the chance to be named the Monster Energy NASCAR Cup champion.

Drivers who qualify for the Chase are given extra points so that drivers outside of the Chase will not be able to beat their final score. This point system ensures that the Monster Energy NASCAR Cup winner will be one of the 16 Chase for the Cup drivers. However, because of the extra points awarded to those drivers, the winner will not be determined until the last race, or even the last lap.

Martin Truex Jr. has had 19 career wins in the Monster Energy Series.

Elliott Sadler has had three major wins in the Monster Energy Series since starting as a rookie in 1997.

NASCAR organizers want all drivers to race competitively through the end of the season, even if they are not part of the Chase. To encourage this, racers who do not qualify for the Chase have chances to win other awards. For example, throughout the season, the winning driver of each race will receive a cash prize. During the final championship event, the highest-ranking driver that is not a part of the Chase wins a bonus of about $1 million in prize money, among other honors.

RESEARCH AND DEVELOPMENT

NASCAR has worked to keep the sport competitive while keeping the costs of competing under control. Crashes sometimes occur, so NASCAR created many safety measures to help prevent injuries. The NASCAR Research and Development Center is a 61,000 square foot (5,567 square meter) testing facility. There, prototype cars are tested by crashing them into walls at different angles. Additionally, the cars are set on fire, pushed, pulled, and dragged to test the strength and durability of the body, tires, engine, and safety equipment. Parts used in NASCAR racetracks are also tested. This includes the "soft" barriers along racetrack walls. They are made from a webbing of steel tubes that are filled and covered with rubber to absorb impacts.

The Main Event

Several activities that lead up to the main event take place the week prior to the Monster Energy NASCAR Cup race. On Monday, the teams check that all of their gear arrives and is ready for the race. Drivers have the day off.

On Tuesday and Wednesday, the cars are tested. Drivers take the cars out onto the track to learn how to adjust the vehicles so they ride well on that specific course. The crews make changes to the cars. On Thursday, drivers complete practice runs and work with the teams to get the cars ready for the qualifying events.

On Friday, drivers take part in qualifying races for one of the 36 spots in the final event. Another six spots are open to drivers who may not have had a fast time but have enough points to qualify. A final spot is reserved for a past winner of the Monster Energy NASCAR Cup who would not qualify otherwise. Drivers complete one or two laps around an empty track, driving as fast as possible. Drivers with the best times qualify to race in the final event.

Race day is Sunday, and the main event begins with the sponsor's meeting. Race fans get a chance to meet the drivers and ask questions. Before drivers get into their cars, they walk across the track and wave to the crowds. The national anthem is played, and a tribute to the military is performed as jets fly over the racetrack.

It costs a NASCAR team about **$400,000** a week to run a car.

While racing, cars get up to **5** miles per gallon. They can go up to **90** miles on one tank of their 98-octane unleaded fuel blend. (8 km, 145 km)

The average pit stop takes between **13** and **15** seconds, in which time the car is refueled and the tires are changed.

At first, cars do warm-up laps to help them establish their speed. Before the actual race begins, all of the moving cars line up in position behind the **pace car**. The race begins when a green flag is waved. A checkered flag is dropped as the winning car and driver cross the finish line. After the race, there is a big celebration in the winner's circle, and the trophy is handed to the winning team.

5 YEARS OF MONSTER ENERGY NASCAR CUPS

YEAR	RACE WINS	CUP WINNER
2018	 3	Joey Logano
2017	 8	Martin Truex Jr.
2016	 5	Jimmie Johnson
2015	 5	Kyle Busch
2014	 5	Kevin Harvick

THE MONSTER ENERGY NASCAR CUP TROPHY

The Monster Energy NASCAR Cup is the top prize in the Monster Energy NASCAR Cup Series. A new trophy was unveiled in 2017. NASCAR worked with the company Jostens on the new design, which took more than 300 hours to complete. The aluminum trophy features the curving outlines of 23 Monster Energy Series racetracks. It measures more than 37 inches (94 cm) tall and weighs 68 pounds (31 kg). The cup can hold almost 4.7 gallons (17.7 L) of liquid, which would take almost 40 16-ounce (473-milliliter) Monster Energy drinks to fill.

Where They Race

N ASCAR races take place throughout the year at 30 unique courses across the continent. These include road courses, superspeedways, and short and intermediate tracks. The Monster Energy NASCAR Cup Series typically features 23 of these racetracks in its annual circuit. Use the map and legend to see which Monster Energy NASCAR Cup racetracks are near you.

Washington

Montana

Oregon

Idaho

Wyoming

UNITED STATES

Nevada

Utah

Colorado

20

California

13

Arizona

New Mexico

2

17

Pacific Ocean

MEXICO

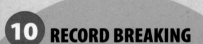

10 RECORD BREAKING

The Indianapolis Motor Speedway has more seats than any other racetrack. It can fit 250,000 NASCAR fans around its track.

Monster Energy NASCAR Cup Racetracks

1. Atlanta Motor Speedway, Hampton, GA
2. Auto Club Speedway, Fontana, CA
3. Bristol Motor Speedway, Bristol, TN
4. Charlotte Motor Speedway, Concord, NC
5. Chicagoland Speedway, Joliet, IL

6. Darlington Raceway, Darlington, SC
7. Daytona International Speedway, Daytona Beach, FL
8. Dover International Speedway, Dover, DE
9. Homestead-Miami Speedway, Homestead, FL
10. Indianapolis Motor Speedway, Indianapolis, IN
11. Kansas Speedway, Kansas City, KS

CANADA

North Dakota

Minnesota

Wisconsin

South Dakota

Michigan

15

Iowa

5

Ohio

Nebraska

Indiana

10

Illinois

12

Kentucky

Kansas

11

Missouri

West Virginia

Virginia **19**

14

North Carolina

Tennessee **3**

4

Oklahoma

South Carolina **6**

Arkansas

21

Mississippi

Georgia

1

Texas

22

Alabama

Louisiana

Florida

7

Maine

New Hampshire
Vermont

16 Massachusetts

New York

23

Rhode Island
Connecticut

Pennsylvania

18

New Jersey

8 Delaware
Maryland

District of Columbia

Atlantic Ocean

9

MAP LEGEND
- United States
- Other Countries
- Water
- # Monster Energy NASCAR Cup Series Racetrack

SCALE

0 miles   360 miles

0 km   580 km

12 Kentucky Speedway, Sparta, KY

13 Las Vegas Motor Speedway, Las Vegas, NV

14 Martinsville Speedway, Ridgeway, VA

15 Michigan International Speedway, Brooklyn, MI

16 New Hampshire Motor Speedway, Loudon, NH

17 Phoenix International Raceway, Avondale, AZ

18 Pocono Raceway, Long Pond, PA

19 Richmond International Raceway, Richmond, VA

20 Sonoma Raceway, Sonoma, CA

21 Talladega Superspeedway, Lincoln, AL

22 Texas Motor Speedway, Fort Worth, TX

23 Watkins Glen International, Watkins Glen, NY

Women in NASCAR

Although most NASCAR drivers are men, women sometimes take part in the sport as well. In 1977, Janet Guthrie qualified to start at the Daytona 500. She was the first woman to earn a spot in the cup series. In the same season, Guthrie raced in the Indianapolis 500. The following year, Guthrie finished ninth at the Indianapolis 500 and posted season winnings of $84,000. Guthrie had her best finish at the Milwaukee 200, taking fifth place. She built her own team and helped to pave the way for other women to take part in car racing events. In 2006, Guthrie was inducted into the International Motorsports Hall of Fame.

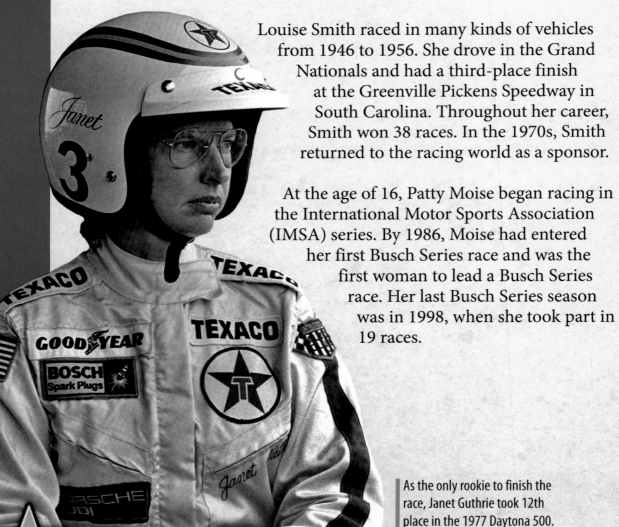

Louise Smith raced in many kinds of vehicles from 1946 to 1956. She drove in the Grand Nationals and had a third-place finish at the Greenville Pickens Speedway in South Carolina. Throughout her career, Smith won 38 races. In the 1970s, Smith returned to the racing world as a sponsor.

At the age of 16, Patty Moise began racing in the International Motor Sports Association (IMSA) series. By 1986, Moise had entered her first Busch Series race and was the first woman to lead a Busch Series race. Her last Busch Series season was in 1998, when she took part in 19 races.

As the only rookie to finish the race, Janet Guthrie took 12th place in the 1977 Daytona 500.

Tammy Jo Kirk also made headway for women in stock car racing. In 1991, she became the first female driver to race in the Slim Jim All-Pro Series. At the end of the 1994 season, Kirk won the Snowball Derby at Five Flags Speedway in Pensacola, Florida. In 1996, she became the first woman to win two Busch Pole Awards in the series. Kirk was also chosen as the most popular driver in the series that year. In 1997, she began competing in the NASCAR Truck Series, winning $134,000 in prize money. Kirk finished seventh out of 29 Truck Series rookies at the end of the season.

In 2010, Danica Patrick joined the NASCAR Nationwide Series. Patrick is the only woman in history to win an IndyCar series race. She also finished third in the 2009 Indianapolis 500, the highest finish ever by a woman. Her switch to the NASCAR circuit brought many new fans to stock car racing. In 2018, Danica retired from NASCAR. There are many new young women in NASCAR working to replace her as the queen of racing.

Danica Patrick first learned to race by go-karting with her family. She went on to compete in almost 200 Monster Energy NASCAR Cup races.

WOMEN IN THE PITS

In 2006, Nicole Addison was the first woman to join a pit crew team. A mechanic and tire specialist, Nicole trained hard for her position as a rear tire changer. Nicole participated in PIT Instruction and Training, which involves eight weeks of physical training, drills, and trials. She worked and practiced until she felt she was good enough to earn her place and make a positive contribution to her team. Nicole's shop duties include installing decals on trucks, ensuring the tires are ready for each race, and making sure there are tires ready for testing the tracks. She enjoys the fast-paced Truck Series and helping her race team win.

Important Moments

Stock car racing is a very dangerous sport. Over the years, NASCAR races have had many terrible crashes. Officials try to learn from crashes to improve safety and prevent future accidents. On May 24, 1964, Glen Roberts was racing at the Charlotte Motor Speedway when he swerved to avoid a crash and hit a gate. In an instant, Roberts's car flipped and caught fire. Roberts died from his injuries. After the crash, NASCAR officials changed the rules so that all fuel cells were rubber lined and almost impossible to puncture.

In 1960, CBS Sports broadcast its first live NASCAR Grand National Division event. For the first time, television viewers were able to see the Grand National Pole Position races from Daytona. Announcer Bud Palmer hosted the first two-hour program that was devoted entirely to stock car racing. By 1983, TV cameras were mounted inside the cars to bring viewers right into the action.

In 1967, Mario Andretti competed in the NASCAR Grand National Division. He won in only his second run at the Daytona 500, making history. Andretti is a legendary and extremely skillful driver who holds many records and has earned several racing accomplishments.

In 1988, Bobby Allison and his son Davey finished first and second at the Daytona 500 race. This incredible finish for the Allison family highlights how generations of drivers have defined the sport. With the win, Bobby Allison became the oldest winner of the Daytona 500.

In 1998, NASCAR celebrated its 50th anniversary. As part of the celebrations, Las Vegas Motor Speedway was added to the season schedule. Mark Martin won the inaugural event at this speedway on March 1, 1998.

Davey Allison competed in the Monster Energy Series from 1985 to 1993. He had 19 wins in 191 races.

In 2010, Jimmie Johnson set a record by winning his fifth consecutive Monster Energy NASCAR Cup. That year, he finished the regular season with 6 wins and 23 finishes in the top 10. He also won in 2013, bringing him to a total of six Cup wins—one win short of the all-time record.

Then in 2016, Jimmie Johnson made history by claiming the Monster Energy NASCAR Cup again. He finished the season with five wins, including the final race at Homestead-Miami Speedway, which he came from behind to win. Johnson joined legends Dale Earnhardt Sr. and Richard Petty, the only other drivers with seven Monster Energy NASCAR Cup titles.

45 years old
Oldest Monster Energy NASCAR Cup Champion
Bobby Allison
1983

7
Most Monster Energy NASCAR Cup Championship Wins
Richard Petty, Dale Earnhardt Sr., and Jimmie Johnson

14 laps
Biggest Lead at a NASCAR Race Finish Line
Ned Jarrett
1965

23 years old
Youngest Monster Energy NASCAR Cup Champion
Bill Rexford
1950

NASCAR RECORDS

157
Most Second-Place Finishes
Richard Petty

0.002 seconds
Closest NASCAR Finishes
Ricky Craven over Kurt Busch, 2003
Jimmie Johnson over Clint Bowyer, 2011

94
Brothers with Most Cup Wins
Bobby Allison (84) and Donnie Allison (10)

18
Consecutive Years with a Win
Richard Petty
1960–1974

Legends and Current Stars

Richard Petty

Richard Petty is called the King of NASCAR for a reason. Over the course of his 34-year career, Petty won the Daytona 500 and Monster Energy NASCAR Cup seven times each between 1964 and 1981. He set numerous NASCAR records, including races won, races started, and money earned. Petty is also part of a racing family, with his father Lee and son Kyle both pursuing racing careers. Following his retirement from racing in 1992, Petty stayed in the racing world. He oversees a NASCAR race team, Richard Petty Motorsports, and a racing garage, Petty's Garage.

Dale Earnhardt Sr.

Racing legend Dale Earnhardt was part of a racing family—his father, Ralph Earnhardt, was a race car driver and mechanic. This inspired Dale to pursue a racing career, too. Before long, Dale earned the nickname "Intimidator" for his aggressive style. This style led him to the NASCAR Rookie of the Year title in 1979 and his first cup championship in 1980. Dale won his first Daytona 500 in 1998. Three years later, he crashed at the end of the Daytona 500 and lost his life. He had won seven championships and set records for career earnings. His son, Dale Earnhardt Jr., has carried on the family tradition of race car driving.

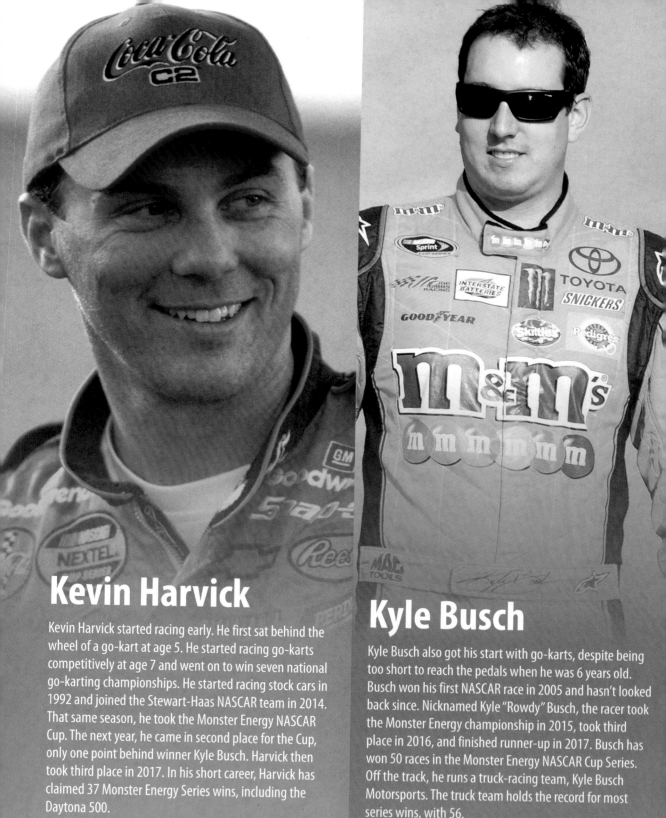

Kevin Harvick

Kevin Harvick started racing early. He first sat behind the wheel of a go-kart at age 5. He started racing go-karts competitively at age 7 and went on to win seven national go-karting championships. He started racing stock cars in 1992 and joined the Stewart-Haas NASCAR team in 2014. That same season, he took the Monster Energy NASCAR Cup. The next year, he came in second place for the Cup, only one point behind winner Kyle Busch. Harvick then took third place in 2017. In his short career, Harvick has claimed 37 Monster Energy Series wins, including the Daytona 500.

Kyle Busch

Kyle Busch also got his start with go-karts, despite being too short to reach the pedals when he was 6 years old. Busch won his first NASCAR race in 2005 and hasn't looked back since. Nicknamed Kyle "Rowdy" Busch, the racer took the Monster Energy championship in 2015, took third place in 2016, and finished runner-up in 2017. Busch has won 50 races in the Monster Energy NASCAR Cup Series. Off the track, he runs a truck-racing team, Kyle Busch Motorsports. The truck team holds the record for most series wins, with 56.

All-Time Records

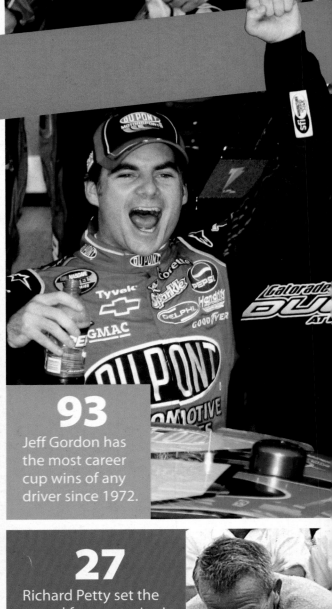

93

Jeff Gordon has the most career cup wins of any driver since 1972.

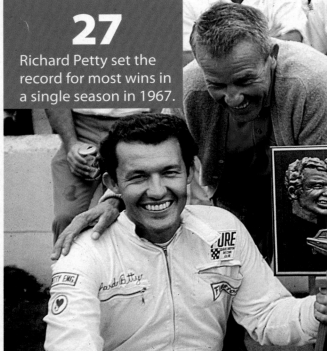

27

Richard Petty set the record for most wins in a single season in 1967.

38

Bill Elliott competed in the Monster Energy NASCAR Cup for 38 years from 1975 to 2012.

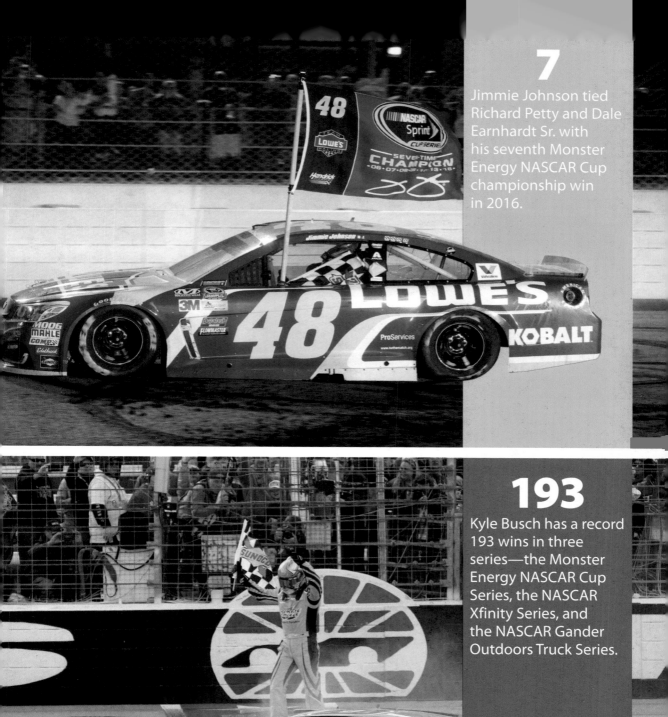

7

Jimmie Johnson tied Richard Petty and Dale Earnhardt Sr. with his seventh Monster Energy NASCAR Cup championship win in 2016.

193

Kyle Busch has a record 193 wins in three series—the Monster Energy NASCAR Cup Series, the NASCAR Xfinity Series, and the NASCAR Gander Outdoors Truck Series.

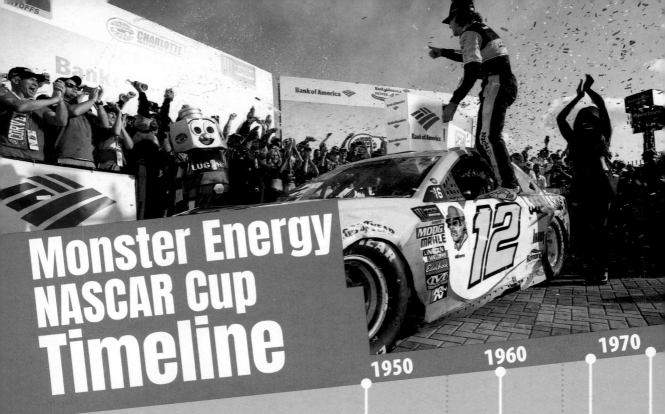

Monster Energy NASCAR Cup Timeline

1950 1960 1970

The history of the Monster Energy NASCAR Cup is filled with spectacular victories, devastating losses, and tragic crashes. Today, the series continues to evolve as one of the most prestigious competitions in NASCAR. Some of the most significant events and defining moments of the Cup's history are plotted on the timeline.

1947
Led by Bill France, the Strictly Stock car racing league is formed at Daytona Beach, Florida. Within a year, the first official NASCAR race is held on the Daytona Beach Road Course.

1959
The first Daytona 500 takes place at a new racetrack that will come to serve as the world center of stock car racing.

1967
Formula One driver Mario Andretti races his first stock car to victory at the Daytona 500.

1971
The Grand National Cup becomes the Winston Cup. The series bonus prize money increases by $100,000.

28

1978

Dale Earnhardt Sr. debuts at the Charlotte Motor Speedway as a last-minute replacement. Two years later, he wins the series championship.

1994

Dale Earnhardt Sr. matches Richard Petty's championship record by winning his seventh Monster Energy NASCAR Cup.

2014

NASCAR requires all race cars to reduce their **horsepower** from 850 to 725. This reduces the engine's power, meaning a car cannot go as fast. The reduction is meant to improve driver safety.

1980 **1990** **2000** **2010** **TODAY**

2001

A crash ends the life of racing legend Dale Earnhardt Sr. in the final lap of the Daytona 500. Because of the tragedy, NASCAR adopts stricter safety regulations, including making a head restraint mandatory for drivers.

1987

Bobby Allison crashes his car. It launches into the air and lands in the stands. After the crash, new safety rules are put into place.

2018

Joey Logano takes the Monster Energy NASCAR Cup Series title after crossing the finish line 1.725 seconds ahead of Martin Truex Jr.

Today

NASCAR continues to be one of the most popular sporting organizations in the nation, with the Monster Energy NASCAR Cup Series, the NASCAR Xfinity Series, and the NASCAR Gander Outdoors Truck Series.

1 In what year was the Chase for the Cup playoff format adopted?

2 How many inspections do NASCAR officials conduct of each car entered in the race?

3 When was the first organized stock car race held in the United States?

4 What is a NASCAR helmet's visor commonly made of?

5 Where is the first race of the Monster Energy NASCAR Cup Series held each year?

10 QUESTIONS To Test Your Knowledge

6 Who was the first female driver to compete in the Monster Energy NASCAR Cup Series, and when did she first compete?

7 Who was the first woman to join a NASCAR pit crew team?

8 All metal parts in a NASCAR car must be made of which metal?

9 How did Kevin Harvick and Kyle Busch get started in racing?

10 Which driver has won the most races in a single season?

ANSWERS

1. 2004
2. Five
3. 1936
4. Bulletproof material
5. The Daytona International Speedway
6. Janet Guthrie in 1977
7. Nicole Addison
8. Steel
9. They raced go-karts as kids
10. Richard Petty

Key Words

aerodynamic: shaped to move quickly through the air

asphalt: man-made surface of a racetrack

banking: sloping roadway

clutch: a pedal that disconnects the engine from the transmission

compression ratio: a number that is used to predict how well an engine will perform

horsepower: the power of an engine

manufacturing: creation or construction

officials: people who are in charge of how a race is run

pace car: a car that sets the position of the cars on the track and the pace for the race

pit crews: people who work in an area on the side of a racetrack where cars are serviced

treads: patterns on a tire's surface which give it grip

unmodified: not changed from its original state

wheelbase: the distance between the front and back wheels on a car

Index

Log on to www.av2books.com

AV² by Weigl brings you media enhanced books that support active learning. Go to www.av2books.com, and enter the special code found on page 2 of this book. You will gain access to enriched and enhanced content that supplements and complements this book. Content includes video, audio, weblinks, quizzes, a slide show, and activities.

AV² Online Navigation

Book Pages
AV² pages directly correspond to pages in the book.

Audio
Listen to sections of the book read aloud.

Video
Watch informative video clips.

Key Words
Study vocabulary, and complete a matching word activity.

Embedded Weblinks
Gain additional information for research.

Quizzes
Test your knowledge.

Slide Show
View images and captions, and prepare a presentation.

Try This!
Complete activities and hands-on experiments.

AV² was built to bridge the gap between print and digital. We encourage you to tell us what you like and what you want to see in the future.

Sign up to be an AV² Ambassador at www.av2books.com/ambassador.

Due to the dynamic nature of the Internet, some of the URLs and activities provided as part of AV² by Weigl may have changed or ceased to exist. AV² by Weigl accepts no responsibility for any such changes. All media enhanced books are regularly monitored to update addresses and sites in a timely manner. Contact AV² by Weigl at 1-866-649-3445 or av2books@weigl.com with any questions, comments, or feedback.